Prayers that Sing
&
Stir the Heart

W. Sibley Towner

UNION
PRESBYTERIAN
SEMINARY
For the Church in the World

Chief Editor: Beverly Zink-Sawyer
Assistant Editors: Clay Macaulay & Celia Luxmoore
Student Assistants: Rebecca Heilman & Rosy Robson

Union Presbyterian Seminary is the federation of Union Theological
Seminary (founded in 1812) and the Presbyterian School of
Christian Education (founded in 1914 as the Assembly's Training
School for Lay Workers).

Cover Photo: "Rappahannock Sunset" by W. Clay Macaulay

Proceeds from the sale of this book will benefit
Union Presbyterian Seminary.

Contents

Foreword

In exemplary fashion—with characteristic diligence, compassion, wisdom, humility, and effectiveness— W. Sibley Towner has fulfilled his vocational call to Christian ministry through his many contributions to theological education.

As an esteemed professor and Dean of Faculty (at both Dubuque and Union Presbyterian seminaries), he epitomized the accolade he received as a young instructor at Yale Divinity School: "Friend of Students." His versatile productivity as a biblical scholar includes insightful commentaries on three dramatically different Old Testament books: Genesis, Daniel, and Ecclesiastes. He excelled as a teacher of exegetical theology and homiletics, and also as a preacher himself—able to bring witnesses of scripture to fresh understanding and applicability.

But former colleagues and students alike will recall especially the literate poignancy of the prayers he offered at the beginning of his seminary classes and on many other occasions. Sib's public prayers were always delivered from the heart, revealing his deeper sensitivities and commitments. Yet they were also works of theo-poetical craftsmanship—carefully designed to focus minds and imaginations in lifting up shared praises, joys and sorrows, and petitions to the Deity.

Sib's prayers could be bold and provocative—though, as a man of peace and consistent benevolence, he never traded in guile, polemic, or anger. His prayers were eloquent, but did not waste words. They were typically succinct—even epigrammatic in their rhetorical strategy—exhibiting a delight in striking vivid, "well-turned" phrases that shone like gold jewelry (Proverbs 25:11). I can't imagine that the Divine addressee hasn't appreciated them, too.

The contextual timeliness of the occasions for which these prayers were composed and delivered will be evident to those who read them today. Still, they retain their original qualities of gracefulness and pleasant surprise as they nurture our personal and corporate relationships with a providential, loving, life-affirming Creator. They are a welcome part of the legacy of one who has responded faithfully by enriching the lives of others in acknowledgment of the precious life he has been divinely given.

Well done, Sibley—servant of the Word, loyal colleague, and cherished friend.

S. Dean McBride Jr.
Professor Emeritus of Bible
Union Presbyterian Seminary

Prayers that Sing and Stir the Heart

According to Luke 11:1, Jesus' disciples asked him to teach them to pray. Rather than launching into a discussion of the meaning of the transaction we call prayer (as I am about to do), Jesus did what they asked. He taught them the Lord's Prayer.

Before and after teaching his prayer, however, Jesus offered three revealing comments on prayer. First, he warned, "Do not heap up empty phrases as the Gentiles do; for they think they will be heard for their many words" (Matt. 6:7). Are we to picture God stifling a yawn as a lengthy Gentile pastoral prayer floats into the divine receiver, or is Jesus talking about what is going on in the minds of the verbose senders? I think it is the latter, for the concern in the Lord's Prayer itself and in two of the three surrounding instructions is largely with the inner life of the praying community. "Keep it short and precise," this seems to be saying; verbose and confused praying suggests conceptual ambiguity, and conceptual ambiguity leads to inattention and (even worse) inaction. Even Islamic prayer, which occurs five times per day, is supposed to be kept short. Mohammed taught that Allah prefers less talk and more action on behalf of the poor and the oppressed.

This instruction seems to me to be Jesus' endorsement of the editorial blue pencil. However, I do not think it is a suggestion that all prayer consist of gruff monosyllables and blunt appeals. No. Judging from the brief yet eloquent model prayer that follows, Jesus means that prayer which is conceptually clear and structurally precise is also most likely to meet the deep human need for beauty in expression—something for which, I believe, people are starving. Because public prayer undertakes to "deprivatize" the messages that the community of believers wishes to send to God, it should do so as clearly and beautifully as possible, so that the believers can give warm emotional assent to what they have said through the liturgist.

Secondly, Jesus goes on to give a reason for his critique of verbose prayers. "Do not be like them, for your Father knows what you need before you ask him" (Matt. 6:8). This is the one teaching that Jesus offers in this passage about what kind of God it is who receives our prayers. God already knows, so why are we bothering to pray? Why, for *our* sakes! We are doing it to create a spiritual and mental world around ourselves, up to the measure of which world we can then seek to fit ourselves. To the degree we succeed in doing so, we are changed, we grow into the stature of Jesus Christ, and we become a different force in the world.

All of this flows from the prior initiative of God, who, in the words of the Psalmists, in the great prose prayers of David and Solomon and Ezra, in the cry of Jonah from the belly of the fish, and, above all, in the words of Jesus, taught us how to pray, what to pray for, and what values to underscore in prayer. Walter Brueggemann has argued quite eloquently that prayers like Psalm 100 ("Know that the Lord is God! It is he that made us, and we are his...") created the kind of world for Israel and subsequently for Christian communities that could stand firm even as the tyrant's goons came in the back door and down the aisle. The community that could pray like that knew that God, not the tyrant, was king.

Of course, in the real world, the tyrant *might be* king, and the goons could and often did proceed to break the liturgist's teeth and herd the congregation into waiting boxcars. Prayer creates a world that in reality doesn't exist. Prayer creates a new world quite other than (let us even say *finer than*) the real world in which we live day to day. It is God's gift for survival—for survival with integrity, for growth. It is a means that God has given us by which there may be convergence between what we think we need and what God knows we need. Prayer creates a world far more value laden, far more spirit filled—far bigger than the real world. And that is good, because it is only as human beings can begin to grow into the stature offered by that larger world that we can hope to transcend the bleak realities that could break us here.

Thirdly, the NRSV/RSV translation of Matt. 6:12 differs from what we usually recite in church. It reads, "And forgive us our debts, as we also *have forgiven* our debtors." This use of the English past perfect tense implies that something has already happened on the side of the community before ever the prayer for forgiveness of sins was offered. Jesus comments on this implication in the verse that follows the Lord's Prayer: "For if you forgive men their trespasses, your heavenly Father will also forgive you" (Matt. 6:14). Prayer that is not deeply interrelated with action is not effectual at all, and the action should be the constant action of a style of life and not simply a deed done after the prayer has been heard. That means that prayer is only one part of the training in and practice of discipleship. It is less a pious duty (Hebrew *mitzvah*) than it is a continuous exchange involving the praying community, the wider world, and Sovereign God.

Having said all of this theoretical stuff, let me state several convictions of a practical nature:

   a. The beauty of the ancient prayers of the church can hardly be surpassed. The prayers of the church fathers and the Reformers and the *Book of Common Prayer* have stood the test of time. They have become part of the fabric of our faith and even our language, and often they are still the best vehicles for the deprivatization of the hopes and fears of the worshiping community.

   b. There is a place for surprise and even touches of humor in prayer. The surprise may well come in apt but non-traditional metaphors about God which the prayer uses, or the unexpected concreteness of the way in which the word-images of the prayer seize upon the real world around us and recast it into the world into which God wants us to grow up. And humor can evoke amused recognition of our shared humanity or bring smiles of delight regarding God's marvelous works and ways.

c. But the line between attractively artful and deceptively artificial is a fine one. Too much humor, too much provocative concreteness, too much clever flirting with novelty or heresy can become merely eccentric. Then the prayer no longer speaks for the community, but only attests to the whims and conceits of the liturgist. As with other forms of public speech, the "prudent" liturgist will use restraint in the choice of prayerful words (Prov. 10:19).

With these thoughts in mind, I offer these prayers in the fervent hope that they may serve as useful examples in our quest to offer prayers to God as we, too, learn to pray as Jesus taught his disciples. And by offering to God these and other prayers that sing and stir the heart, may we grow closer to God and to each other—and to realization of the vision of the kingdom for which Jesus taught us to pray.

W. Sibley Towner

Editor's Note from Beverly Zink-Sawyer:
It is with much joy and thanksgiving that we share
this collection of beautiful prayers composed by our
dear friend and colleague W. Sibley Towner. Most of
the prayers were prepared for use at the opening of his
Old Testament class sessions. A generation of students
who attended Union Presbyterian Seminary had the
privilege of hearing Dr. Towner invoke the blessing
of God upon their daily activities of study and worship,
work and play. Upon the occasion of his retirement in
2001, one of his former students, the Rev. Gary Charles,
spoke for many others when he said, "Some waited for
his sermons like fine entrees prepared to perfection.
I waited for his prayers that began each class with
language that sang."

The prayers are presented here as Dr. Towner wrote
them, including some specific and outdated references.
It is our hope that the use of these prayers in public
and private worship may indeed stir the hearts of
yet another generation of faithful Christians, and we
echo the wish of colleagues in the Communications
Office whose retirement tribute concluded, "So here's
to Sibley Towner, a mentor and friend. May your legacy
continue. May your words never end."

The Bible and the Hebrew Language

Thanks to God for the Bible

O God, your word to us has always come in human form. How else could we have understood your commandments and your promises? How else could we have glimpsed the winsome ways of Jesus and heard him say in plain English, "Follow me!"

Heavenly voices wouldn't have worked. They never do. Ecstatic experiences among lamps and incense would have left most of your children cold. Books handed down from heaven would have been found out.

No, your word to us is a treasure in the earthen vessels of ancient manuscripts with scribal errors, in modern versions printed in funny squiggly characters, in CD-ROM programs. We thank you that your words always point to the Word made flesh: Jesus, our Lord, whom we know also as the Spirit who moves within our hearts to answer questions and to make things clear. AMEN.

The Canon

O God, under the inspiration of your Spirit, you guided
the canonizers to gather up all the scattered oracles of
the prophets, the epigrams of the sages, the legends of
the beginning, and the stories about Jesus into one book.

Nothing was ever the same after that. No longer could
we read about Eve without thinking also about Mary,
nor contemplate the suffering of the Servant of Yahweh
without also sharing in the suffering of Mary's son.

You made us a people of the book—the whole
book—and so gave us unbounded riches of story and
letter and vision, divine gifts to the imagination—all
the wonderfully interwoven tapestry of the written
Word of God. Thank you for the canon of scripture.
AMEN.

Study of the Torah

O God of Abraham, Isaac, and Jacob—for generations now, our ancestors in the faith have searched for your word in the words of the Torah:

> Some squinting in the dim light of flickering lamps in the Judean caves;
>
> Some standing in the cold of stone monasteries before books chained to their desks;
>
> Some peering through thick lenses as they rocked and read before their ghetto shops;
>
> Some in furtive glances at the book hidden above the bunk at Auschwitz.

O God, it is our turn now. Keep us faithful, we pray, to so great a heritage.

In the name of our Rabbi and Friend, Jesus of Nazareth. AMEN.

Genetics Goes Awry

You founded this world upon the seas. You established it upon the floods, O God. And scripture assures us that you will leave it there.

Oh, sure, we have messed up before, and there have been tragic consequences. Scripture tells us that, too. In fact, you give us no reason to think that we might not mess up again, with equally tragic consequences— blistering, parching consequences—consequences which, if we do it to ourselves, we must bear. For you never said, O God, that you would ever uncouple the human deed and its historic consequence. You are too just and too sure for that.

But the scripture also assures us that it is your promise that you will never again destroy the earth. You have promised that the sun will shine and the rain will fall and the bees will pollinate and the worms will aerate and the marsh grass will shelter the eggs of the fish and all of the wonderful, providential, life-sustaining orders of the world will go on and on—because you want them to.

O God, thank you for your promises. They give us the framework in which to make peace. They make real the possibility of peace, and the reality of peace they make exquisitely worthwhile. AMEN.

(See Genesis 8:31-32.)

Ancestors

O God, we marvel sometimes as we look over our
spiritual genealogies to see how it happens that
we believe in you. There are the recognizable figures,
to be sure—the giants of the faith: Abraham, who
came within a second of cutting the slender thread
that tied him to us, his sons and daughters; and Moses,
our lawgiver; and Ruth, the righteous gentile; and
Mary. And there are those special figures, too—those
skeletons in the spiritual closet: the men and women
with strange lights in their eyes. Some of them saw
you face to face, O God, or saw your chariot flash by.
Some had tongues of fire dancing on their heads. Some
preferred to die rather than to spit on a single title of
your law. Some went out into the desert to build there
a little model of the city of God.

We don't know what part each of the visionaries and
martyrs and saints may have played in shaping our
faith. But we thank you for all of them, and thank
you that our faith is rich, not bland—and far from
boring—and that it throbs with holy energy. AMEN.

(See Genesis 12.)

God the Elector of Abraham

O God the Elector, who chooses aged women and ruddy-cheeked shepherd boys to enact great chapters in the history of our salvation, and who decided upon a peasant girl of Nazareth to be the Mother of God, we praise you for your choices. We praise you for their magnificence and their audacity. We praise you for choosing Abraham, the uncircumcised pagan from Iraq, to inaugurate a dynasty which also includes your anointed one, our Savior. O God, choose us, too—unlikely as we may be.

Raise us up as sons and daughters of Abraham so that we may enjoy the promises and stand at the cutting edge of your plan to bring blessings to all the nations of the world. AMEN.

(See Genesis 17:1-21.)

Flawed Joseph and Flawed Brothers

O God, you used Joseph's amazing technicolor dreamcoat to accomplish your purposes through him. Jacob seemed dense—without good sense—for making only one robe, not 12. For his part, Joseph almost botched it with all his bragging and prancing around in his beautiful kaftan. The green-eyed brothers also cut a sorry fratricidal figure as they swished the dreamcoat in the blood of a goat.

But through all this swirl of emotions and foolishness, you worked quietly and steadily to save your people. Therefore, we have faith that you can find your way through our well-intentioned efforts and our occasional compulsiveness, too, and incorporate them all into the work of your reign on earth. AMEN.

(See Genesis 47.)

No Other Gods

O God, those who call you Allah say you have 99 names, but they do not begin to know you in all the ways and by all the names by which you can be known. Neither do we. We have never experienced you as an immense void, but others have. We have never brought our spirits into union with yours through the slow whirl of the dervish dance, but others have. We have never seen you in a cow or a snake, nor in fire, but others have — and have experienced the reality of your presence.

Therefore, give us humble hearts and sharp ears, O God, so that we who call you Yahweh can learn from others even more about who you are. AMEN.

(See Exodus 20:3.)

The Rise of David

Your word to us is always incarnate, O God—fleshy, bawdy, adventuresome. You give us the shepherd boy with the fastest slingshot in the east, the handsome court musician who soothes Saul and sings sacred psalms. You give us David, the mercenary soldier, the insurgent, the political operator, the maker of alliances in bed. And precisely this flawed hero, O God, you make the king with the great vision, the founder of a line that has no end, the ancestor according to the flesh of Jesus of Nazareth.

Truly, you give us treasure in earthen vessels, O God, and we earthen vessels thank you for it. AMEN.

(See 1 Samuel 16 – 2 Samuel 8.)

God's Amazing Choices

O God the Elector, who chooses humble midwives and ruddy-cheeked shepherd boys to enact great chapters in the history of our salvation, and who decided upon a peasant girl of Nazareth to be the Mother of God, we praise you for your choices. We praise you for their magnificence and their audacity. We praise you for choosing the House of David to inaugurate a story of messiahs (anointed kings) whose end we have not heard even yet.

O God, choose us, too, we pray, and help us to be strong right and left hands in the court of the anointed one. In His name, we pray. AMEN.

(See 2 Samuel 7:1-17.)

Before Reading the Psalter

You have always led the singing, O God—even for a generation that had lost all hope of national salvation. For persons who were sick, you recommended psalms of praise and thanksgiving, just as you did to those who wished to praise you from their hearts. You gave us a rich treasury of psalms and spiritual songs.

O God, may the grimness of politics in our generation never drive away the sound of melody. And may the austerity of our scientific reasoning never squelch the deep cries of joy which well up from the inmost soul.

In Jesus' name, we pray. AMEN.

The Road to Wisdom's House

We come to you, O God, for a city map—the route to wisdom's house. You set wisdom before us in the guise of a lovely lady who loves those who love her, and who endows those who find the way to her with true wealth: the golden fruits of righteousness and justice, knowledge and discretion.

Guide us to wisdom's house, we pray, O God, and usher us into the doorway of she who is your first creation—your delight, your love. Then can we know you more clearly, honor you more nearly, and handle our own restlessness and dis-ease with more quiet poise.

In Jesus' name, we pray. AMEN.

(See Proverbs 8:1-31.)

God's Word Abides

Your word, O God, abides. Human empires rise and fall, but your word of assurance, O God, abides. Our personal monuments last a while, and then they wither away, and we are forgotten. But your word of comfort, O God, abides. Before we finish the work we set out for ourselves to do, we make our rendezvous with destiny. But your word, O God, abides.

Thank you for being God. AMEN.

(See Isaiah 40:1-8.)

Overview of Ecclesiastes

O God, you put in the world billions of images of yourself, and endowed us all with astonishing brains by which we experience joy and suffering in an incredible spectrum of colors. How could we ever have imagined we could acquire fixed answers to all the human questions about meaning, about justice—about you, O God? Lest we fall into shallow thinking and facile speaking, you sent us Job and Qoheleth to teach us to look again, to dig deeper, to be content with no pat answers but with the knowledge that you are God and that life—in all its messiness and vanity—is your good gift to us.

Thank you, God, for those wild and crazy guys, and for Jesus, who shows us the way through the chaos named the Via Dolorosa. AMEN.

The Teacher's Inconsistencies

The Teacher doubts we can ever find wisdom, O God. The Teacher also teaches that wisdom gives life to the one who possesses it. Darn that Teacher, God! Why did he speak with forked tongue? Why did the Spirit inspire synagogue and church to consider his inconsistencies to be Holy Scripture?

Because there is truth in both sides of what he says, you say? Because his skeptical mind was needed to balance the confidence of those who felt they knew exactly what you would do?

But let us not fall into that very trap ourselves. We don't know why you gave us Ecclesiastes. Furthermore, the world is chaotic, and we don't know the outcome, but we trust you to be God and to be good, and, by golly, we're going to keep seeking wisdom—especially the wisdom of your word—no matter what! So there! AMEN.

On Beginning a Course
on Biblical Apocalyptic Literature

O God, Alpha and Omega, Creator and Re-creator,
we strain to look ahead, but we cannot see clearly.
Sometimes we think we catch a glimpse of the shining
towers of your city. Other times, we see only boiling
smoke and tumult. Little by little, God, we have learned
that the path runs in only one direction—ahead—and
that we must take it. Little by little, we have learned
that we have no map to guide us—not even within the
pages of the Holy Book. Little by little, we have come
to realize that no one—perhaps not even you—can say
what will befall us.

But this we do believe—yes, we know it, God—that
you walk the path, too, as Immanuel, and that you will
be there with us as we confront the turnings and the
terrors on the way. You shrink back from nothing—not
even a cross. O God, Alpha and Omega, Savior of this
age and joy of the age to come, help us to trust and to
work as hard as Jesus did out of love for this wonderful
world and its beautiful human creatures. In His name,
we pray. AMEN.

Myriads Around the Throne

O You who we cannot know in yourself—whose
glory hides you from our poor eyes—we thank you
for giving us the privilege of metaphors. To speak
of thrones and myriads and streams of fire would be
to talk nonsense, except that you have chosen words
and a Word through which to share yourself with us.

Thank you, God, for your blessing of word images.
In the name of the richest image of all, our incarnate
Lord. AMEN.

(See Daniel 7.)

Prayer Upon Commencing
a Study of the Prophets

O You who does nothing without first revealing it to
your servants the prophets, grant us insight into your
purposes for ourselves and our church and our nation,
we pray. We ask this not because we seek to invade
your hiddenness, but because we hear the distant road
grow louder and so, for your people's sake, would
prophesy. In Jesus' name, we pray. AMEN.

(See Amos 3:8.)

Treasure in Earthen Vessels

We might have chosen some other way, O God, to
disclose the truth about you and the human condition.
The words of the Bible seem so foreign sometimes—
so ancient, so childlike. Yet we acknowledge how
superior they are to thunderclaps and heavenly voices
and mystic trances—not to mention learned
dissertations—because they ring true to life. They
are understandable. They are vivid and even fun.
They are, like your Son, our Lord, incarnate words—
very human and very godly at the same time.

O God, you have given us treasure in these earthen
vessels. Thank you! AMEN.

(See 2 Corinthians 4:7.)

Law/Liberation

We might have preferred only Gospel, O Lord, but
you gave us law, by which we might give shape to
our amorphous freedom.

We might have preferred only Grace, O Lord, but you
gave us justice, as well, so that we might never delude
ourselves.

We might have preferred only Love, O Lord, and indeed
love lies in the very arms of all you give us.

Thank you, O God. AMEN.

History

You meet us in real time, O God, and you exalt our plain old history into saving history. You taught us the meaning of faithlessness when Ahaz blinked before the Syrians. You tested Hezekiah and found him faithful in securing the walls of besieged Jerusalem. You moved Haggai to move the elders to rebuild your temple in 515.

That was real time, O God. You were there when they crucified our Lord on Friday, and you transfigured all of human history when a man who was not dead tenderly greeted his women friends on the third day afterward.

You meet us in real time, O God, and history is never meaningless again. In Jesus' name, we pray. AMEN.

The Significance of the Hebrew Language

O God, who sanctified the Hebrew tongue by speaking through the storytellers, the prophets, and the sages to your people Israel in their own language, consecrate, we pray, our tongue, as well—and the languages of all peoples—to the holy task of proclaiming the history of your saving acts and the joy of your salvation. AMEN.

On Studying the Niphal Binyan

Lord, we praise you for the falling of Niagara and
the whirling of the turbines, the leaping of the deer,
and for our own energy and vitality.

But we thank you also for the passive voice and
for times of passivity.

We are glad we can ask to be quieted, to be secure,
to be satisfied. We know it is important to love, but
we are glad also to be loved.

As for Hebrew, we ask not to be spared, but to be
enlightened. AMEN.

Use of the Past

O God, by whose Spirit the church lives in every
generation and in every place, teach us the proper use
of the past. Give us that combination of integrity and
quietness of mind which will enable us to expound
your scriptures well and truly, and forgive us when
we deal falsely and lightly with the text. In Jesus' name,
we pray. AMEN.

First Meeting of Hebrew Class

O God, we might have done it differently, had we been you. We might have chosen a language with vowels and question marks and nice nasal consonants. We might, for example, have chosen English. But we are not you—thank you, Lord—and you have made your choice.

Help us embrace your word as tenderly as we would embrace you. Give us diligence and sharp, swift pencils and a wry enjoyment of the unexpected.

In Jesus' name, we pray. AMEN.

On Studying the Hiphil Binyan

Lord, First Cause of all that is, Igniter of the Big Bang:

In the beginning, you caused light to shine out of darkness and dry land to rise out of the sea. You caused plants to evolve into the beautiful mums and tasty tomatoes that grace the lives of your sentient creatures.

In the end, you will make all things new and you will cause the river of life to flow for the healing of the nations.

We are glad that you, O Creator, make things happen, and we thank you for the gift of hiphil, so that we can talk more readily about you as Prime Mover and Prime Shaker. AMEN.

The Hithpael

O God, you have taught us that the wages of sin are death, and that the one who lives by the sword shall die by it. We learn that a reflexiveness is built into things, so that our deeds produce their own destinies. We hurt ourselves when we disrespect you or cheat our neighbors.

Help us get smart. Help us learn to launch motions in our families, our churches, our country that go around and come around to good. Help us to bless ourselves by blessing you and others. Help us to love in ways that feed back grace and not scandal.

We thank you that we have the language to talk about this reflexiveness. Maybe we can at least comprehend the depth of it.

In the name of Jesus Christ, who did not spare himself and so spared us. AMEN.

Speaking Urdu

O You who manifest yourself to us in words and
who appeared Incarnate in our midst as the very
Word of God, we praise you for the human capacity
for language. Dogs may sniff and butterflies may sip,
baboons may bellow and whales sing, but we—your
most gifted creatures made in your image—we speak
Arabic and Urdu, Tagalog and Swahili, English and
Hebrew.

With words, we can evoke tears and laughter. We
can cause riots and overthrow Babylon. Best of all,
we can enlist our words in your cause, and so we do,
Lord. You have our word. AMEN.

The World/Creation

Creation by God's Word

Nine times you spoke, O God, and it was done and it was good. We don't know how you did it. Maybe you sent an asteroid crashing into the primeval soup. Maybe you did it all with amino acids. We don't know how you did it. We only know that the heavens have never finished telling your glory, and that the earth still shows your marvelous creative handiwork.

What new surprises do you have in store for us, O God? What will your 10th word be? AMEN.

Cosmology: The Alliance of Science and Religion

O God, whose truth is manifest to those who have eyes to see it in the swirl of the galaxies, in the tiny symmetry of the seashell, and in the words of the holy book, grant us the discipline and wit to remain in holy discourse with science and technology. And grant, we pray, that our nerves never fail us before the awesome tracery of the atom, or before the awesome totality of the gospel. AMEN.

(See Genesis 1.)

Through Evolution God Creates Us

O Creator God, worker of wonders with the stuff of the cosmos, you took carbon and oxygen and nitrogen and what-have-you and formed a little earthly image of your holy self and called us good. You teased us out of the primeval slime and gave us a place a little lower than the angels. You worked with the hot-blooded mammals of the Eocene and the Pleistocene until, in the slow turning of Providence, you remolded their fangs and furry snouts into the soft skins and gentle eyes that meet ours and fill us with joy and desire.

We praise you, God—you wondrous artist with chemicals and genes! And we thank you for the vocation you have given us, the most favored of all your creatures, to serve you by loving each other and the other living creatures with whom you have gifted us to share this beautiful world!

Arouse in us, O God, a providential creative passion of our own so that we may assist you in your creative work by caring for our world, by admiring and nurturing our fellow creatures, and by giving thought for those living beings more beautiful and intelligent than we—more like you—who will succeed us here.

In the name of Jesus, who loved women and men and little children and, if not behemoths, at least the lilies of the field. AMEN.

(See Genesis 1:26.)

The Image of God's Creativity

O God, you imagined your whole creation—right down to the serpent and the sweetgum tree, the lion and the lamb, the cucumber and the apple. Then you created it all with your warm words of love. Above all, you lovingly made us and put in us your very image—lips that can speak your words, minds that can learn your will, and bodies that can do it.

And we can do it, God. Once, we were children and were dependent and lacking wisdom. But you have entrusted to us adult responsibilities now: the safety of the lion and the lamb and the sweet apple trees, the condition of the topsoil and the purity of the water, the integrity of human relationships, the formation of the outlooks of children, and the honor and care of the aged.

And, O God, you have given us rules, as well, about how to get on with your great work—rules of truth and fair play, reason and honor, trust in your power and in our powers, and, above all, love.

O God, keep our love for you as warm as yours is for us, that our imaginations and our brains can glorify you. AMEN.

(See Genesis 1:26.)

Confessing that the Image of God is No Light Thing

To bear your image in ourselves is no light thing, O God. Your justice in us may take us where we fear to go. Your love in us may drive us closer to each other than prudence dictates. To be your viceroys in this place may plunge us into awesome responsibility.

But so it is written, and we bless you for having created us in your own image.

In the name of He who gave his image its most comely human form—even Jesus Christ, our Lord. AMEN.

(See Genesis 1:26-28.)

Image in the Other

O God, you made us in your own image and asked us to rule the earth on your behalf. The ruling part is fine. We can handle it. It's the image part that's scary, because you can only mean that if we look deep and long into the thin faces of the refugee and the cancer patient and even into the kindly, careworn face next to ours, we will see you there. AMEN.

(See Genesis 1:28.)

The Little Clay Doll

O God, you lifted us up out of the soil of our origins and made us creatures in your own image. You made a little clay doll and breathed into it the breath of life and said, "Tend my garden."

Help us do it with intelligence and skill, O Lord. Help us discharge your assignment in a way that brings life and happiness to others. Let us be peacemakers, Lord, so that, through us, parents and children may find reconciliation, business associates may learn to trust one another again, and nation may not lift sword against nation, neither study war anymore.

All of these things we ask in the name of Jesus of Nazareth, who loved women and men and little children and sparrows and the lilies of the field—and welcomed them all into the fellowship of his kingdom. AMEN.

(See Genesis 2:7.)

Let Us Thank the Creator
for Our Own Creativity

O God, Good Creator, with the basic ingredients of the earth—a pint of light, a dash of darkness, a peck of clay, and some mist—you fashioned the willow tree and the grey squirrel, the hippopotamus and the earth creature Adam. You made the earth creature in your own image, and from it you derived beautiful man and strong woman. When you were through, you saw the meaning of it all and you pronounced it good.

We thank you that you have placed within us your image as creator, and that it abides in our hearts to this very day. We pray for the wit and the courage never to stifle it, but to shine it back to you, our creator, with works of our own creativity—beautifully built and cared-for churches, lovely flower beds, poetic words, diatonic scales, and well-designed curricula.

It is our prayer to you, O God, that in this way—the way of artisans and writers, singers and preachers—we, too, may come to know the true shape and worth of things. AMEN.

(See Genesis 1:26 and 2:7.)

Geography

O God, creator of the world and of all its fauna and
flora, its ridges and hollows, you must love to look
at us. You must have relished maps and charts as you
worked. You put Paradise between four rivers—Pishon
and Gihon and Tigris and Euphrates. You inhabited
your holy mountain not far from Rephidim, just beyond
the Wilderness of Sin. You encouraged your servant
Solomon to build you a house with cedar from Lebanon
and gold from Ophir. You met your truculent escapee
Jonah in a hurricane some miles east of Tarshish.

You never did anything in a vacuum, God. You did
it all right here on good old terra firma—our home.

Where will your next adventure with us be? At the
corner of First and Main? AMEN.

(See Genesis 2:10-14.)

The Sign in the Sky

O God, wherever we look in the world around us,
we see your signs—signs that you are our creator
and signs of your providential care. The distant
supernovas bespeak the continuing dynamism
of the cosmos, and Lucy, the fossil Australopithecus,
shows the care you have always lavished on our
species. The geese in flight signal the slow turning
of the seasons, and the nursing mother demonstrates
the endurance of human tenderness.

These are signs of your love.

So, too, is the rainbow in the sky.

Help us to restrain our waste and abuse of the
environment, O God, so that the rainbow's sign
of providence never goes unseen on a used-up and
empty planet Earth, but always assures whales and
osprey of their safety and always gladdens the hearts
of your human comrades here. AMEN.

(See Genesis 9:13.)

Scarlet Threads in History

O God, you wove the story of Israel with scarlet threads. In and out they go, the warp into which the woof of history is given: David and his house, the anointed one, the people of God.

O God, we sense that the scarlet threads run on out of Israel's story—on and on—and are crafted into the story of Jesus and into our forebears' stories and into our own. On and on they come forever, those scarlet threads, and they mark the way of your future.

Thank you, Weaver of the human story, for working us into the design, somewhere between "A" and "W." AMEN.

(See 2 Samuel 7:1-17.)

When the Morning Stars Sang Together

We come to you, O God, in search of wisdom. Not strange, inhuman wisdom—nor the secrets of the abyss, nor the manner of the end, nor the meaning of your awful silence, nor the melody which the morning stars sang together on the first day. No, God.

We come in search of wisdom that will make us glad in the world—resolute in hope, instant in warmth and love, blameless and upright. Not cursing, but loving you, O God; not dying, but living mirrors of your light and truth. AMEN.

(See Job 38:7.)

Triumph of Men on the Moon

O You who made human beings a little lower than the angels and crowned us with glory and honor, we thank you for the honorable and glorious capacities which you have placed within us, and for the challenges of the world—and even of the whole cosmos—by which they are drawn out. Only draw out more, O God—and soon, we implore you—of our capacities at self-understanding, at loving, at living in peace. AMEN.

(See Psalm 8:5.)

Thanksgiving Prayer: The River of God

O God, from whose throne runs the river of life bright
as crystal, give us hearts thankful for the fertility,
the greenness, the growth of life wherever it runs.
The Psalmist speaks truly for us, too: "Thou visitest
the earth and waterest it, thou greatly enrichest it;
the river of God is full of water." AMEN.

(See Psalm 65:9.)

General Overview of Wisdom

O God, we wonder sometimes where you are. Our
ancestors heard your voice in the thunder's roar, or
in the rustling grass heard you pass. Others saw your
hand at work in the fall of kingdoms, the liberation
of slaves, the works of your outstretched arm.

We are not sure where to look for you now, though
sometimes we glimpse your face in the careworn face
next to ours. In worship and prayer, music and art,
we sense your presence. As far as your mighty acts, are
you telling us they are entwined with our own? AMEN.

Like the Beast, We Must Die

O God, you made us fearfully and wonderfully well
and gave us the most remarkable organ in all the
animal kingdom: the human brain. But we remain what
you made us even so—creatures of the earth—and to
the dust of the earth we shall return.

You gave us the capacity to see great distances with the
mind's eye—to dream dreams. Yet you also placed us
within a world of orders that we must obey. And one
of those orders is that we must die. It's not your fault,
O God, and we're not mad at you. We wear out, like
every other creature.

O Loving God, help us to live fully and richly while
we live; to enjoy our work and our loves; to savor the
sunshine, relish the rain, and learn to whistle the songs
of the meadowlark and "Godspell." Help us to join
you in your work of creation. And when the day comes
that we cease to exist as living organisms, enroll us,
we pray, in the ministry of your kingdom. And let it
be lively, Lord. Let it be lively!

In Jesus' name, we pray. AMEN.

(See Ecclesiastes 3:16-22.)

For Justice, for the Widow

The wretched of the earth are not just lying in the ditches of Delhi or on the Metro grates in Foggy Bottom. You know that, O God, and so even do we. They are in our midst here, too—thumbing their way down the roads; living in unheated, unlit shanties in the woods. Some of them are abused. Some are abusers. Some live in nice homes, too, and share our values, but their demons make them hard to bear.

You can bear them, for they are your children. Help us learn to bear them, too, O God—for they are our fellow human beings, and, like us, they are elected by you into the life of the Kingdom of Heaven. AMEN.

(See Isaiah 1:17.)

Prefiguring the Peaceable Kingdom

O God, who helps us know who we are by showing
us what we shall become, we thank you for the
promise of your Kingdom. We do not know the way
there, we confess. Only you know. Yet the light of
that vision helps us pick our way—around the pitfalls
of selfish pride, narrow sectarianism, and nationalism.

Thank you for the vision of a world without tears,
where justice is achieved and wolves dwell with lambs.
Help us live that way of peace now, and so prefigure
and proclaim that possibility. And hear us, O Lord,
as we join with the saints of all the ages to cry, "Even
so, come, Lord Jesus!" AMEN.

(See Isaiah 11:1-9 and Romans 5:12-21.)

The Crocus in the Wilderness

Almighty God, who speaks through the mouth of the
prophet about a crocus blooming in the arid wilderness
of your judgment, give us eyes to see the first blossoms
of promise—tiny flowers of hope that appear in
our own time in the midst of the ruins of our titanic
schemes.

In Jesus' name, we pray. AMEN.

(See Isaiah 35:1.)

Sleeping in the Woods

The trees yield no fruit in a world that is nuked. We know that, O Lord. No one sleeps in the woods when they're full of hoods. No one lies in the grass under clouds of poison gas. We can hardly remember what a really peaceful, secure world was like, O God—nor do we know how to get there again. It seems so much trouble; it takes so much energy to pursue peace. Sometimes the peace of the grave seems almost preferable.

But your promise won't leave us alone. It pulls us forward—that portrait of the world as it ought to be and will be, that peaceable kingdom of wolf lying down with lamb, with the walls of hostility all broken down. And, yes, there we are, too—a blessing in the midst of the picture. Energize us with your promise, O God. Make us covenanters in your covenant of peace.

In Jesus' name, we pray. AMEN.

(See Ezekiel 34:25.)

The Pleiades and Orion

O God—you who made the Pleiades and Orion,
Gemini and the North Star—you made us, too, out of
stardust, and called us into fellowship with you. We are
not part of you—not little "godlets" sharing the divine
substance—but we are yours, and we bear your image.

What a tragedy it is, then, when we turn our backs
on the maker of all things as if we were sovereign
here, not you. The evil we do lashes back on us and
produces its own destiny, and you weep. Don't sing
your dirge over us yet, O God, we pray. We'll come
around. Honest, we will. AMEN.

The Face of Jesus

You saved the day for us, O God, when you elected to enter our history in the person of a child. In him, you gave us your face. Without him, we might have thought of you as just a big old scary wizard in the sky—frowning and shouting, playing magic tricks on history, and throwing lightning bolts and cancers on people you didn't approve of. We might have thought of you as Oz the Terrible.

But you saved the day when you showed us your face. We are deeply moved to see that yours is a face as innocent as ours was in infancy. We are shocked to see your face surmounted with a crown of thorns. We are glad to see your face radiant with a smile of love.

When we saw you at last in Jesus, we somehow sensed that, even though everyone else in the whole world will forget one day who we ever were, you will remember and be glad. AMEN.

(See Luke 2:16.)

Science and Religion

O God, whose truth is manifest to those who have eyes to see in the swirl of the galaxies, in the words of the holy book, and in the tiny symmetry of a mountain flower, grant us the discipline and wit to remain in holy discourse with science and technology. And grant that our nerve fails us not before the awesome tracery of the atom, nor the courage of our culture before the awesome totality of the Gospel. AMEN.

The Passage of Time

Every Saturday, when I wind our old Seth Thomas mantel clock, I feel the passage of time, O God. Perhaps it is good that the clock keeps ticking though—to remind us that we haven't got forever. Help us turn our time to good account in acts of loving-kindness, in caring for others, and in praising you for the many blessings of life—even the humble, humdrum ones.

So may we glorify you every waking hour, seven days a week—whether the time be Standard or Daylight, Eastern or Central, or Greenwich Mean! AMEN.

The Rhythms of Creation

O God, at the beginning of time—before the Big Bang, perhaps—you put in place the great rhythms that govern the universe. Never mind dark matter and black holes and things we can barely understand. The rhythms and orders that matter most to us are the season of snow and ice, the appearance of the crocuses, the raucous departure of the geese, the human impulse to till the soil and plant tomatoes.

God, give us grace to live peacefully within your orders, respecting the high place you have given us, but knowing that we, too, like all of your creatures, are caught up in the rhythms of your devising. AMEN.

Rich Diversity

O God of all peoples—mother of the Aleuts, father of the Zulus, and emperor of India—we know you have created us to live together in rich diversity. You must have rejoiced in it, for you made us speak so many languages and wrapped us in so many colors. But you also created us to live in peace.

Grant to the vast patchwork nations of the world the wisdom to survive political collapse, and give them the vision necessary to move step by step toward the age of shalom.

In Christ's name, we pray. AMEN.

Mondays

O God, we thank you for the rhythms of our lives.
We thank you that gorgeous autumn yields to bleak
midwinter, and that Advent leads to Christmastide.
We thank you for the gift of weekends—for early
bedtimes sometimes, and partying others—and for
church, and rambles in the woods. And we thank you
for the gift of Mondays—for getting back into the
swing of things, hard work, and high responsibilities.

We would die if life was always the same, like a smooth
plain or a glassy sea. You are our savior from boredom
and aimlessness.

Thank you, God. AMEN.

About the End of History

Dear God, we thank you for the majesty of your design
of the cosmos. We do not know where all of the outer
limits are, or whether the buzz that we get on the radio
telescope is the last echo of the Big Bang or not. Yet
it hints of sublime beauty and order; therefore, it hints
of you.

We thank you also for the majesty of your design in
human history. We do not know how it works, what
went before, or what comes after—or whether the
scarlet threads that run through it are yours or ours.
Yet it hints of the self-destructiveness of evil, of a
prevailing power of good and a moral order; therefore,
it hints of you.

These things we can affirm most of all because of what
we see in Jesus Christ, the person at the very center
of the cosmos and the very center of human history.

In him, we see a way of life that affirms the created
order in all of its details, and the worth of people,
and the beauty of love. We pledge ourselves to live
lives modeled on his, and to keep on hoping the
impossible hope that we shall share in his resurrection
and so experience at last all that we ever had the
potential to be.

You have told us to look ahead to such a time when
this world will have been freed from its bondage
to decay and death. You have encouraged us to live
as though that day will actually come, and to model our

lives and our community and our humanity on
that resurrected community of the Lord.

So here we are, God—hanging in space and in
time between a beginning and an end, between
a resurrection and *the* resurrection, between
a life-giving preview of life in the Kingdom and
its full manifestation.

Help us to not just "hang in there," but to seize the
hour. Help us to live fully; to love earnestly; to go out
into the streets—into the slums, across the seas, into
the labs, into the computer centers—with enthusiasm
and with this word: "There is hope."

Help us to go with this word: "There is freedom to
be fully human."

Help us to go with this word: "Evil is damned!"

Then help us to build—brick by brick, stone by
stone—a new human community that looks as much
as we, seeking your help, can make it look like the city
of God.

Finally, after we have struggled, suffered, worked,
rejoiced, and loved a new humanity into being—and
thus have used the time you have given to us—even
so, then come, Lord Jesus. AMEN.

Both Sides of Our Brains

O God, you supervised our evolution into the species with the marvelous brains.

With the left half, we can:

remember the ancient past; and

think with discipline and depth about it.

With the right half, we can:

imagine; and

make pictures

You gave us people like the yahwist and the gospel writers and Michelangelo and Walter Brueggemann, who brought their brains together in order to render in vivid living images the past, the present, and the future of the people of God.

O God, help us to use our brains—our whole brains, our synchronized brains—to picture your goodness and greatness in words that move and gladden the church. AMEN.

Faith, Family, and Festivals

The Human Family After the Flood

The very earth on which we walk is rich with the
bones of the peoples who have walked before us,
O God. You meant it to be that way. You meant that
human life should spread outward from its origin and
grow ever more diverse. You meant that human culture
and speech should be handed down from generation
to generation and that each generation should add new
discoveries of truth to the lore of the human family.

Our forebears have handed the torch to us. Help us
pass it on, burning brightly. AMEN.

(See Genesis 10.)

Fathers and Mothers Who Have Gone Before

Before you, O God, all the generations rise and
pass away, and they await your pleasure—even the
blessed morning of the resurrection of the dead and
the renewal of the whole creation. But behind them
they have legacies, and for those legacies, we thank
you: genetic legacies, reservoirs of strength and health;
spiritual legacies, which have come down to us from
our own mothers' knees and from the hymns and
writings of the church; intellectual legacies of art and
music and literature; legacies of memory and tradition
of all kinds. We are the heirs of all this, O God.

Give us the sense, we pray, to preserve it with
tenderness. Give us the wit, we pray, to pass it on
to those who are coming after us, enhanced by our
own best efforts. AMEN.

(See Exodus 20:12.)

Hear, O People

Hear, O people of God! The Lord our God, who has
it all together, can help us pull ourselves together, too.
Our God can help us gather up the scattered fragments
of our loyalties and focus our distracted souls. Our God
will make us whole when we love God with all our
hearts and minds and souls. In Jesus' name, we pray.
AMEN.

(See Deuteronomy 6:4-6.)

Portraits of David and Jesus

O God, you have set before us the portrait of good
king David—not only as an example of faithful
obedience and courage, but also as the father of
a dynasty.

O God, you have set before us the portrait of
Jesus—not only as an example of faithful obedience
and courage, but also as messiah ben-David.

Show us now, O God, where we belong in your
continuing messianic purposes, in company with
our beloved David and our dear Jesus. AMEN.

(See 2 Samuel 7:1-17.)

David, Bathsheba, and Solomon

O God, you filled David with the gift of courage,
and into Bathsheba you poured the strength to be
the mother of a king. Solomon, you filled with great
wisdom, and upon the anointed one of David you
poured courage, strength, and wisdom greater than
all of these.

As we take our stand in him, O God, help us draw
deep from this great reservoir, so that we may find
the courage, strength, and wisdom necessary to impose
meaning on our lives. AMEN.

(See 2 Samuel 12:24-25.)

On Not Cursing God

We who have suffered little deprivation and little torture
love you, O God, who have suffered much—even up
to death on a cross. When our time comes, nourish us
by your love, we pray, so that we can bless, not curse,
you—and so that whether we live or die, we do so to
your glory. AMEN.

(See Job 2:9.)

A Few Good Women

O God, this world needed a few good women, and you gave us lots and lots of them. You gave us strong, brave women like Judith and Deborah and Eleanor Roosevelt. You gave us daring women like Esther and Mary Magdalene and Hildegard of Bingen and Rosa Parks. You gave us beautiful, passionate women like Susanna and the Shulamite and Juliet and Eloise. You gave us wise women, to follow the ways of Dame Wisdom herself. You gave us warm, nurturing women like the wonderful lady who rings out the Book of Proverbs, and many another mother and grandma, as well.

We thank you, God, for women in all their colors and personalities and enthusiasms and excellences—for your great cloud of female witnesses.

In the name of He who loved Mary and Martha and the other Mary, and whose life was enriched by theirs. AMEN.

(See the Book of Esther.)

The Outskirts of His Ways

People in every generation have pursued you to find
you and know you, O God. We thank you for the
record of their pursuit. That they have touched bits of
your power and heard faint whispers of your truth is
a joy and triumph. Now help us enter into your mystery
for the sustenance that will nourish our generation.
AMEN.

(See Job 26:14.)

God Speaks Out of the Whirlwind

O God, Yahweh of old, El Shadday—whose glory
is blinding, whose presence is a whirlwind of power,
and yet who can speak personally and kindly to
Job—convey to us, too, we pray, a quiet confidence
in your presence with us. We ask this not because we
would become familiar and cozy with you, but because
to be apart from your strength is for us to be derelict,
as if we were on a dunghill! AMEN.

(See Job 38:1.)

Hearing with the Ear, Seeing with the Eye

O God, for the moments of ecstasy in which we perceive your goodness and your justice, we thank you:

in the creek outside the house, where the whiteness of your lovely swans cleanses the mildew off our imagination;

in the nursery, when the tender touch of the parents on the little baby's face and body reopens the springs of our compassion;

when the heartfelt understanding of a foreign friend once again breaks down the dividing walls of hostility between us.

We had heard of imagination and compassion and understanding with the hearing of the ear, O God. Now we thank you for bringing them before us face to face.

In Jesus' name, we pray. AMEN.

(See Job 42:1-6.)

In Response to Ecclesiastes

O God, who hides yourself from time to time in inscrutable majesty and remote divinity, prepare us for those epochs in which the old symbols fall silent and those hours in which our favorite doctrines take on a dull and hollow sound. Then grant us patience to wait for your word and acuteness in the sense that we have nowhere else to go but to you.

In Jesus' name, we pray. AMEN.

(See Ecclesiastes 1:1.)

Prayer for Lovers/Wedding

O God, you made this world just about right. You gave to the creatures ways of finding each other: so that the owls are never lonely in the dark woods, so that the lions are proud to be part of the pride, so that the apple blossoms reach out and touch each other through the good offices of the bees. Into the human heart, you have stirred the warm leaven of desire, so that the bread of love that we serve each other can be full and delicious.

Like life itself, love is a gift—your gift to us and our gift to pass on to each other. How true is the teaching of the sage that if we offer all of our fame and our fortune in lieu of love, the offer would rightly be scorned. AMEN.

(See Song of Solomon 8:6-7.)

With Wings as Eagles

We grow weary in well-doing sometimes, O God.
We try to do our studies, read all the books, keep up,
do well, get honors. But sometimes we just get fed
up. We'd love to "mount up with wings like eagles"
sometimes, O God. We try to fly high with our children,
soar with our spouse above everything that is grubby
and mean, always be truthful about our feelings with
ourselves. But sometimes we crash.

It's hard to imagine being ministers, having to listen
to complainers and gossip and party strife and then
getting sucked into it ourselves. Help us to give
ourselves and our well-doing over to you, Lord,
who alone "does not faint or grow weary," whose
"understanding is unsearchable"—who alone does
really well! AMEN.

(See Isaiah 40:27-31.)

God's Servant

O God, it looks as if your chosen one, Israel, had plenty to fear. Your servant was crushed, exiled, oppressed. Yet you took their right hand in your big tender hand and said, "Do not fear, I will help you."

Can it be that your choice of whom you love is unbreakable? Can it be that you will never turn your back on your people?

Can the saying be true: "If God is for us, who is against us?" (Rom. 8:31)

Hold our hand, O God. It feels good—and safe, too. It makes us less afraid. AMEN.

(See Isaiah 41:8-13.)

Suffering Servant

O God, we don't know exactly of whom the prophet was speaking when he described one who was wounded for our transgressions and by whose stripes we are healed. But you gave that suffering servant to us as a model by which to measure our lives forever after.

And when we see a corpsman run out onto the battlefield to rescue a wounded soldier, or a nurse bringing the gentle touch to a ward of AIDS victims, or a parent going through rehabilitation right along with a troubled child, or Jesus hanging on a cross— we know that your servant has been there. AMEN.

(See Isaiah 52:13-53:12.)

Holidays

What have you got against our holidays, O God? Our Thanksgiving feast is to your glory, after all, and Christmas is rich with carols celebrating your name.

"Nothing," you say? "Nothing as long as they give us the strength to get up and do what needs to be done"? Okay, God, we get it. You like the happy faces and the gifts, too, but mainly you want action so that more and more faces are happy.

We'll try, God. Honest, we will. AMEN.

(See Amos 5:21-24.)

Ezekiel's Call

O inescapable God—who called Ezekiel beside the
river Chebar in Babylon, who encountered the prophet
Jonah on his way to Tarshish, and whom the Psalmist
discovered even when he made his bed in Sheol—we
have learned from our spiritual ancestors not to try to
run away from you.

It will be a surprise, of course, O God (but help it to
be a joy, as well, we pray), when we hear your still,
small voice in the middle of the night, or perceive the
meaning of your call to us in a blinding flash of insight
at the supermarket, or learn at last the meaning of your
loving-kindness from the soft hand that touches ours.

In Jesus' name, we pray. AMEN.

(See Ezekiel 1-3.)

A Prayer About Jonah's Prayer

Out of the depths, your servants have cried to you,
O Lord, and you have heard their voices. From the
depth of despair, the Psalmist cried, and you were there
and answered with compassion. From the belly of the
fish, Jonah cried, and you were there, and you delivered
him to complete his mission to Nineveh. Along the
wilderness trail, pioneer explorers prayed to you, and
you strengthened them for their journey to the western
Indians. And on the cross, our Savior, Jesus, cried
to you and said, "My God, my God, why hast thou
forsaken me?" That cross was real, and that pain was
stark, but you hadn't forsaken him, and you sent him
on his mystic errand to preach the gospel three days
in the belly of Sheol.

So when we cry for help, assure us of your loving
presence, we pray, so that we, in turn, may be loving
presences and heroes and preachers and even, if need
be, martyrs for you. AMEN.

(See Jonah 2.)

The Waiting Game

Give us the faith by which we may live, O God, while we await the fulfillment of your purpose. And since we have to wait while the vision tarries, teach us how to wait dynamically — ever building, ever thinking, ever active in loving — so that, because of us, the coming victory can be sensed and felt in the air. AMEN.

(See Habakkuk 2:3.)

Lilies of the Field

O God, our Savior and Friend, Jesus, directed our gaze to the lilies of the field, which neither toil nor spin, and yet are more beautiful than Solomon. We know full well that trust, not anxiety, brought us here, and that faith, not fear, enables us to cope.

Even though we know that, God, we still are anxious — every one of us — sometimes. A lot of times. You love us anyway and will never leave our sides. Thank you for that. AMEN.

(See Matthew 6:28.)

Teach Us to Pray

You invited us to talk to you, O God, but it is not easy. People who have loved you all their lives weep when they have to pray to you. People who bless you with every breath of their lives can only mumble incoherently when they are asked to bless the bread and meat. People who call on you in the dire straits of the foxhole or on the deck of the sinking ship can only think to say, "Now I lay me down to sleep."

Why is it sometimes hard and embarrassing to pray, O God? Teach us how to pray in the peace and trust of intimacy with you. AMEN.

(See Luke 11:1.)

Divine Communication

O God, who shows us every day how profoundly our world stands in need of the gospel, we confess our continued membership in the land of Babel—the land of confusion of speech, of ghettos and division and enmity. Give us the Pentecostal power of communication in every tongue and at every level, so that Babel can be undone at last. AMEN.

(See Acts 2:4.)

The Gift of Courage

O God, we thank you for the gift of courage which
you have given all of us in some measure:

> The courage to accept a vocation;

> The courage to leave off doing one vocation and
> start doing another;

> The courage to make our mouths form the words
> of another people's language;

> The courage to spread our wings and fly.

Without that gift of courage and daring, O God, we
would soon be half-dead, even though we were still
alive. Give us grace, O God, to live our lives to the fullest
and then, at the end, to die with no regrets. AMEN.

Thanksgiving Acknowledgement

The landscape of our lives is strewn with your blessings, O God. We acknowledge them:

a Bible full of a rich legacy of insights about you and your work in the world;

a whole library full of books through which we are allowed to enter into fellowship with our fathers and mothers in the faith;

teachers and colleagues who push us, anger us, love us, and never leave us alone to creep off into fruitless corners;

fellow students in the prime of their physical and mental powers, beautiful in their persons, and eager for all that we can share together of our faith.

For so remarkable a landscape in which to walk day by day, we give you our thanks, O Lord. Help us to stick together and not get lost amid the blessings.

In Jesus' name, we pray. AMEN.

Clarity of Conscience

You are not the backseat driver in our minds, O God.
You are not trying to grab the wheels of our lives and
run them for us. That we know from the witness of the
scripture and from the ministry of your Son, our Lord,
in our midst.

You want to sit in the front seat with us, in warm
fellowship. You want to offer counsel and guidance,
and you trust that we will accept it. Then, rejoicing
in all the freedom which you have entrusted to us,
you want to sit back and let us drive.

Give us the maturity and strength to accept such great
trust from you, O God, and give us the wisdom to
know that when the warning lights blink on, you are
there. AMEN.

Independence Day

More than 11 score years ago, our ancestors brought
forth on this continent a new nation, O God, dedicated
to the proposition that all people—men and women
alike, black people and white people and yellow
people, the aged and the young, the gifted and the
specially gifted, the straight and the gay—are created
equal by you.

Oh, maybe our ancestors weren't so inclusive in their
vision of democracy and their sense of justice, but
they'd be proud that you've helped us come as far as
we have. O God, thanks to the prodding of your Spirit
and with help from your church, Independence Day
is a day of gladness for more of our people than ever
before.

O God, the hope for freedom and equality before the
law burns in the hearts of people everywhere—in
China, in Poland, in the West Bank, in Chad and Chile.
Can it be because you planted it there? Can it be that
you covet for every people an Independence Day?
AMEN.

God the Liberator

O God—ruler of the world and all its peoples, ruler
of Seoul and the Straits of Hormuz, ruler of Red Square
and of the Ellipse, ruler of our life together as a church,
ruler even of our agenda—we praise you for your
rule, because it sets us free. Your rule sets us free from
human tyrannies great and small—even those of our
own making—for we answer to you, not to them.

O liberator God, launch us out into the future—even
the future as close at hand as this very afternoon—in
the way you know we have to go, and we fear to go:
without a map; without a timetable; without a tidy plan;
without any certainties whatever, save the all-important
certainty that you intend to launch out with us, ready
to get bruised with us and ready to kick back and enjoy
at the end of the day.

O Immanuel, thanks. Thanks. Thank you. AMEN.

Wedding Prayer

O God, you made this world just about right. You gave
to the creatures ways of finding each other: so that the
owls are never lonely in the darkened woods, so that
the lions are proud of being part of the pride, so that
the apple blossoms reach out and touch each other
through the medium of the bees. Into the human heart,
you have stirred the warm leaven of desire, so that the
bread of love which we serve each other can be full
and delicious.

Now we thank you that (N. and N.) have found each
other and today are making a covenant together.
On their behalf, we lift up many petitions to you.
Give them steadfastness and adventure alike, so that
they can embrace the trials of their life together and
render a good account by the very way in which they
overcome. Let them give each other good counsel.
May their marriage be such a statement of their faith
in the power of love that men and women can gesture
in their direction and say, "Look! That is what life is like
in the Kingdom of Heaven."

If the gift of children should be theirs, guide them
in the awesome task of parenting. So will a new line
of the (N. and N.) families be a blessing to us all, just
as (N. and N.) are in their generation.

We are all implicated in what happens here today,
O God. We know that very well. With the enthusiastic
exchange of new vows, we remember our own
significant others, and our own promises to keep.
May we all find our own family ties strengthened,
and depart from here refreshed in the freshness of
(N. and N.).

Grant that the human qualities which bind us to one
another be so transformed by your Spirit that love may
reign in our hearts, and peace and justice in the earth.

Through Jesus Christ, our Lord, we pray. AMEN.

Offering Prayer of Dedication

These gifts are yours now, O Lord. They always were, actually, but you placed them in our keeping for a time. Now we surrender them to a cause greater than ourselves, to be used as you direct the church by your Spirit—in wondrous acts of healing, in deeds of help and kindness, in the creation of beauty in music and art, in proclaiming to all the world the good news that God loves us before ever we find our way to God.

In Jesus' name, we pray. AMEN.

Benediction

Weave the pieces of life together

on the loom of God's love;

and in word and deed,

create new things all your lives long.

And may God lead us to enact here a community of such peace and acceptance that passers-by will point our way and say, "Look! That is what life is like in the Kingdom of Heaven!" AMEN.

Palm Sunday

O God, whose dearly beloved Son was greeted by the crowd as he came down the road from Olivet with cheers and palm branches, but who, in the same week, was mocked and spat upon only a few blocks away as he staggered up the road toward Calvary: Help us, we beseech you, to keep the road into our hearts open for him. And let him enter in there not to be crucified again, but to find there a glad response of loyalty and love and discipleship. Through the same Jesus Christ, our Lord. AMEN.

Monday of Holy Week

Almighty God, whose Son did not know his first joy without first suffering pain, and did not enter his glory before he was crucified: Save us at this season, we pray, from a facile gladness and a cheap Hosanna—as though we could reach the scene of the Easter triumph by any other road than the way of the cross. AMEN.

Easter's Hero

O God, whose power to bring life our ancestors discovered in flowers and eggs, in rain and thunder: We thank you that, behind all the symbols and metaphors, we discover you to be our own risen and living Lord. And, O God, we confess that, having learned that, nothing is the same anymore.

In the name of Easter's hero. AMEN.

Festival Season

We thank you, O God, for the festival calendar of our faith, for the rhythm and structure it gives our lives, and for the renewal of life, of hope, and the courage to be—which it brings us at this season. AMEN.

Eastertide

O God, whose Son did not reach the scene of his Easter triumph without passing along the Via Dolorosa:

saveus at this season from any cheap Hosannas or sappy Hallelujahs,

but let them well up from the depths of our own life experience and our doubt.

Then faith can truly call out to faith. Then can the ascent of Calvary become for us, too, a rising-up to meaning and fulfillment.

In Jesus' name, we pray. AMEN.

Christmas

Let us speak to God about children at Christmas:

How wonderful it is, O God, that the great festival of Nativity is so open to the imaginations and hearts of children. There they stand, in vulnerable wonder, rank on rank, beside the manger bed, only steps away from their own cribs. When we theologians talk about you, O God, we do so in polysyllabic words and complex formulas. The children who witness to the Nativity need few words at all. They know holiness when they see it. They hear the song of the angels and believe that the baby is the Christ, the Son of the living God. They capture the sense of the candles, the ethereal music, the pretty lights, and know that the thing which has happened is a thing of great importance and bright splendor.

O God, we pray for all children that they may come to know the baby Jesus as the man who takes them in his loving arms.

Let us pray for holy focus at this season:

How easy it is to lose track of what it's all about, O God. Feverish is our struggle to make sure that the Christmas presents look beautiful, that all are satisfied with their gifts, and that Christmas is a happy time for everyone. There's nothing wrong with happiness, of course, O God. And nothing wrong with families coming together—far-flung ones with near-flung ones, grandchildren being reunited with grandparents.

Just keep us focused, we pray, on the knowledge that God loves us all. Then the carols will really sing! Then the gifts will really count.

Let us pray for our own parents:

O God, we who also were once children thank you for the gift of life itself. Our parents conceived us deep in the genetic stream that flows down from our ancestors. They bore us and brought us up as children, wide-eyed at the world around us. They gave us good gifts of food and shelter, love, and encouragement. In this Christmas Present, we thank you for them. We ask you to make us better parents for our own children because of the memory of a warm presence, a soft touch, an adoring word, and the safety of being tucked in bed at the end of Christmases Past.

continued

Christmas *continued*

And finally, let us give witness to the meaning of the incarnation in our own lives:

O God, you chose an unlikely way to come to dwell with us, children of dust and spirit. Other people feel they have experienced you in blinding visions, in the ritual chant of monks singing two notes at once, or in profound silence. We Christians testify that we have experienced you in all the stages of human life, beginning as a newborn baby lying in a feedbox. Truly, you took great risks at Christmas, O God, when you came as Emmanuel, as one of us. Why, you might have died in infancy! Why, you might have been ignored as a young man! Why, you might have been crucified as an adult! But you took your place with us, O God, and so ennobled our infancy, inspired our youth, and challenged our adulthood.

That is why we love you more dearly and seek to follow you more nearly, day by day.

In Jesus' name, we pray these things. AMEN.

Invocation

O God, in whom alone our spirits trust, we invoke
your Spirit's presence in our midst during our time
of intellectual striving. We need your presence,
Lord—not to give what we do here an odor of sanctity,
but rather to give us the wit to savor what is true.

Help us, we pray, better to understand how the
contours of our present lives as Americans have been
shaped by the religious convictions of our fathers
and mothers—and show us how we may, in our turn,
pass the received traditions on to our children with
an enlarged, not diminished, vision.

In the name of He who is our vision and the Lord
of our hearts. AMEN.

Faculty Meeting Prayer

We, whose profession it is to help people find wisdom, pray for wisdom of our own, O God. Please hear our prayers. These three are especially urgent ones:

make our hearts supple to your intelligence, we pray;

even though we know that we must go into the future without a timetable and without a map, give us keen foresight, we pray, into the direction that our church should follow from now on;

endow us with wisdom in the ways of peace, we pray, so that as individuals and as teachers and as members of the Body of Christ, we can join in the vast worldwide search for a new order of equity.

O God, consort of Sophia from the beginning and friend of those who love her still, we open our hearts to your light and truth. We pray these things in the name of the One whom we know to be your Word in our midst. AMEN.

Reformation Day

We remember Martin Luther with gratitude today,
O Lord. Not only did that servant of yours challenge
the whole church to renew its allegiance to you by
putting away its love of money and of political power,
but he respected your people so much that he learned
Hebrew and gave them back their Bible in a beautiful
and faithful German translation of it. Grant us the
courage to take our work of translation as seriously
as he did his. AMEN.

Election Day

In their wisdom, O God, our Founders gave us, the
people of the United States of America, the quadrennial
privilege of replacing and renewing our government.
No need for revolutions or *coups d'état*, palace intrigues,
or tribal warfare. You guided them toward the idea of a
peaceful placement of a piece of paper in the ballot box.

Help us and all citizens this Tuesday, we pray, to vote
with utmost earnestness for the American values of
fair play and opportunity for all, and to promote the
Christian values of faith in the future and love for all
God's creatures. AMEN.

Installation Prayer

O God, you called Moses out of a burning bush and Ruth in the land of Moab and Paul on the Damascus Road, and you told each one, "Tend my flock." Through all the ages of the Christian church, men and women have heard you summoning them to serve you in the preaching of the gospel and in the nurturing and care of others.

Now, at the latest moment in that long history of call and ministry, you have—in your mysterious workings through session and presbytery—brought this servant/ minister to serve your people here. Bless her.* Guide her. Pump her up when she is down. Inspire her to speak your word. Do all this, we pray, so that she may be for us our living Moses and Ruth and Paul. And give us the wisdom to recognize her as a genuine apostle for our days.

O God, we thank you for the gift of courage which you have given all of us in some measure and (N.) in special measure:

> the courage to accept a vocation;
>
> the courage to leave off doing one vocation and start doing another;
>
> the courage spread our wings and fly.

Without that gift of courage, O God, we would soon be half-dead even though we were still alive. Give her the daring to pour out her caring and love on the just and on the unjust, just like you do, and thus to live her life to the fullest.

Lord, we have heard you calling in the night, "Whom shall I send, and who will go for us?"

Here we are, O God—fit and feisty and bushy-tailed. We are ready to go, Dear Friend, if you will lead us. You will lead your people through her. We know her, and we know that she will do that. We know she will touch us and be touched by us. We know she will hold your people tenderly in her hands and in her heart.

In Jesus' name, we pray. AMEN.

The masculine also may be substituted in this prayer.

Commencement Prayer

A Thanksgiving for where we have come from:

O God, who put the solitary into families, and who ordained that every child should sometime have a father and a mother, we bless you for those parents who loved us into being, who sheltered us and guided us along the way, and who, even now—after decades of devotion—are prepared to go the second mile and the second mortgage for our sakes.

At the beginning of our lives, they represented you to us. We looked into their faces, and, behold, you were there. In time, we have come to see them for what they really are: creatures like ourselves. We look into their faces today, and, behold, we are there. But we love them more, not less, for that.

The same goes for family. We feel gratitude and love for them, too. Teach us how to thank them all—in a way that uses words and does deeds, in a way that is tender and is not the least bit corny.

An Ascription for where we now are:

O Source of Life, Light of the Mind, we ascribe glory to you for communities of scholars, students, and teachers, whose task it is to shake us to the very core with the true facts of life. In particular, we praise you for this community of ours, Union Presbyterian Seminary.

Good things have happened to us here, and sometimes we have felt the pains of growth, too, as we have inched up closer to the stature of Jesus Christ. Good, important things happened in the library, when from a book we got an idea that absolutely blew our minds and changed the very direction of our lives. They happened in the seminar room, and in chapel that time a few of us joined in prayer. They happened over lunch, and as we talked into the winter dusk. We have found friends and loved them, and we have exchanged with each other the gifts of our own spirits. Oh, thank you, God, for those gifts, which are surely akin to the gift of your Spirit.

Many of us leave this place now, O God, in eager anticipation of the next chapters in our lives—eager to get on with our work, eager to find new communities of faithful people. But we will never forget what happened to us here.

"Lord, give us faith and strength the road to build; to see the promise of this day fulfilled…"

In the name of Jesus Christ, our Lord, we pray. AMEN.

Alpha and Omega

O God, Alpha and Omega, Creator and Re-creator,
we strain to look ahead, but we cannot see clearly.
Sometimes we think we catch a glimpse of the shining
towers of your city. Other times, we see only boiling
smoke and tumult. Little by little, God, we have learned
that the path runs only one direction—ahead—and
that we must take it. Little by little, we have learned
that we have no map to guide us—not even within
the pages of the Holy Book. Little by little, we come
to realize that no one—perhaps not even you—can
say what will befall us.

But this we do believe—yes, we know it, God—that
you walk the path, too, as Immanuel, and that you will
be there with us as we confront the turnings and the
terrors on the way. You shrink back from nothing—not
even a cross.

O God, Alpha and Omega, Savior of this age and joy
of the age to come, help us to trust and to work as hard
as Jesus did out of love for this wonderful world and its
beautiful human creatures.

In His name, we pray. AMEN.

Discipleship

The Sacrifice of Isaac

I guess most of us don't really think you ever asked any of your servants to sacrifice his son on your altar, O God. None of us would ever expect another believer to go to such an extreme of devotion.

But in our zeal to sanitize your call to us, O God, keep us aware of the North Korean pastors who gave their lives and those of their families rather than deny you. Let us not forget the Dominican priests who died for the sake of their aboriginal flock. Let us not forget the gifts of Archbishop Cranmer and Archbishop Romero and Dietrich Bonhoeffer and the Filipino Christians who resisted the tyranny of the occupiers—and all the others whose faithfulness approached that of your Son, our Lord, and who died that his faith might become our faith, too, and the faith of our children. AMEN.

(See Genesis 22.)

Covetousness

Temper our spirits, O Lord. Fill them with flaming
desire for the cause of justice. In the cause of
peace, let no fuel be left to feed the old flame
of concupiscence—that deadliest of all our sins,
that grabby desire to take all things into ourselves.

May the desire that the other person get a square deal,
that our own obedience to your sovereign will be
pure, and that the creatures may live in safety until you
finally draw them to yourself burn with such brightness
in our lives that people can point to where we are and
say, "Look, the light of the coming Kingdom is breaking
out already!" AMEN.

(See Exodus 20:17.)

On Not Bowing the Knee to Baal

O God, on those days when we feel alone; when
we alone are not bowing our knees to Baal; when
our sense of vocation has to run every hurdle placed
there by criticism, scoffing, and our own second
thoughts—on those days, O God, show us the friends
and the community who really are there and who are
already falling in beside us.

God, thank you for not leaving us alone. In the name
of our Friend and Companion, Jesus Christ, our Lord.
AMEN.

The Lying Spirit

O God, we might have wished that the Hebrew
theologian had put it some other way than imagining
that you would send a lying spirit into the mouth
of the prophets. But we know what he was talking
about. We know that the preaching of the church can
be corrupted, too. We know that war and slavery and
bigotry have lyingly been interpreted as good and just,
and that even the tyrant Hitler could get endorsements
from the pulpit to do his evil deeds.

But we trust you, God. We trust you to send a brave
voice into the midst. We trust that you are Lord even
of the realm in which we lie, and that what we
intended for evil you can weave into the fabric of
your purpose. AMEN.

(See 1 Kings 22:19-23.)

Prince of Peace

Once, you chose a single people, O God, and you gave them a line of anointed kings/messiahs of whom there is no end. Now you have chosen all peoples to be your own inheritance, and you have invited us all to take our stand in the anointed one, the Messiah, who died once for all of us. Now all of us can call your anointed one our own Wonderful Counselor, our own Mighty God, our own King Jesus, our own Prince of Peace.

If all your children have one single prince of peace, then why should we still fight and kill each other? AMEN.

A Prayer Offered When Considering
Our Own Prophetic Ministries

O God, put in our mouths, too, the words of the prophets! O God, give us the bravery and the love to be pluckers-up and breakers-down. O God, give us the imagination, the effectiveness of speech, to be builders and planters. O God, sharpen and make keen our sense of justice. O God, impregnate all we do with good humor and true hope so that the colors of our prophetic ministries are neither pitch black nor crimson red, but are full of warm, vital hues.

We pray these things in the name of he whom the prophets described both as son of man with the two-edged sword and as the suffering servant, even Jesus Christ, our Lord. AMEN.

(See Jeremiah 1:4-10.)

Prophetic Lament

O God—you whose word was experienced by the prophet Jeremiah as a fire within, you whose commission led the prophet into mockery and violence—we dare to ask: Give us more pizzazz and punch!

So often, we are politic and cautious. So often, we cross the road to avoid the crisis. So often, we refuse to take the risk. In a time of apathy and dull religion, give us, O God, some zeal! Please!

In Jesus' name, we pray. AMEN.

(See Jeremiah 19:7-12.)

Showers of Blessing

Your reign among us is nothing if not abundant, O God. It is a pearl of great price; its showers are showers of blessing. The river of life flows through it. May we who minister here among your treasures, your gems, be a blessing and give a foretaste of your reign in the abundance of our faith and the steadiness of our compassion.

In Jesus' name, we pray. AMEN.

(See Ezekiel 34:25-31.)

God Wants Sacrifice, All Right

We always thought we were doing what you wanted, God, when we brought the beautiful gifts to your altar—when we poured out the rivers of oil, sang the great chorales, burned the incense, and offered the fruit of our bodies for the sin of our souls.

What a shock it is to learn that you want a different kind of sacrifice altogether!

It's not going to be easy to sacrifice the will to serve ourselves and the need to be loved more than to love. It's going to be rough to enter into relationship with you entirely on your terms, and not at all on ours.

But what a relief it is to know from your own lips that your favor is not for sale to the highest bidder, and that you will enter with us into partnership in living and loving if only we will yield to you.

In Christ's name, we pray. AMEN.

(See Micah 6:6-8.)

The Servant

O God, who has given to our fathers and mothers in
the faith the vision of a day in which your servant will
make everything right, help us to draw nourishment
from their response to that glorious possibility. We want
neither the smug assurance of the saved nor the bleak
despair of the damned, but the mature purpose of
those who can learn from the future kingdom how
to live and love and work as servants now. AMEN.

(See Zechariah 9-14.)

Jesus on the Cross

O God—who did not spare this man his agony upon
the cross, yet did not forsake him, either—enable us
to face the pain of death, the trials of suffering, the fear
of hostility, the uncertainty of waiting in the very spirit
of our Savior, trusting you to make of tribulation a good
thing through us and to make us examples of hope
and faith.

Let us pray for the church. AMEN.

(See Matthew 27:33-50.)

Jesus' Sacrifice and Ours

O God, when the shepherds and the magi laid their gifts before the Christ child in Bethlehem, they did it for no reason but gratitude and joy. Theirs was a sacrifice of thanksgiving.

Help us to step up to the manger beside them to offer the gift of our gratitude, knowing that, by that act, our whole lives will be caught up in His, our innocence restored, and we will be delivered at last from scheming and disobedience. AMEN.

Pentecostal Power

O God, through the mouth of the Apostle Peter, you taught those who experienced the wonders of the first Pentecost that their amazing speech and their fire were the first evidences of the New Age. We praise you that they had the courage to act on that new faith—to gather together in a community in which bread was broken, prayer was offered, and all things were held in common.

Now give us the courage, we pray, to be a community of believers so committed to one another and to the general good of the human family that people will point to us and say, "Look, the light of God's Kingdom is breaking out already!"

In the name of He who you made both Lord and Christ. AMEN.

(See Acts 2:1-47.

New Jerusalem

Only you can bring history to its conclusion, O God.
Only you can build the New Jerusalem. But you have
given us work to do in the meantime. We get the future
that we deserve, the future that we are constructing
even now.

Give us the integrity, wisdom, and courage to build
a good one — to advance the cause of the poor and
disadvantaged now, to encourage the sad and the angry
now, to help mothers and fathers be nurturing parents,
to egg on doctors and scientists and legislators to
spread good health — in short, to give previews now
of the world as it will be when you make all things new.

It's a big order that you have given us, but we shudder
to think of the alternatives. So, honestly, God, we'll do
our best. AMEN.

Courage to Be Better

O You who answered Moses' prayer for courage,
David's cry for obedience, and Solomon's petition for
enlightenment, hear our prayers as well. Enable us
to live and study and work as befits persons who are
taken up and made one with your Son, who is more
courageous than Moses, more obedient than David,
wiser even than Solomon. AMEN.

Education

We echo the petition of the Psalmist, O Lord: "Make me to know your ways...; teach me your paths. Lead me in your truth, and teach me."
We want to know more of your word for us and your will for us.

O God, we also thank you for giving us that incredible evolutionary adaptation, the human brain, that makes us capable of learning new things, making new connections, and having new spiritual insights until the day we die.

Lord, don't let us miss out on any chance to be further educated! In the name of the one we call Rabboni, our teacher. AMEN.

(See Psalm 25.)

Universal Church of Jesus Christ

For the family within the family of humankind—the church of your Son, our Lord—we thank you, O God. In all the ages, you have set people free through its ministry to become honorable and generous and humane persons.

May it be so in our day, too, Lord. May it be so —we beg it trembling—in our lives, too, O Lord. It is not that we covet the pains or the palms of sainthood, but only the passionate love of Christ. AMEN.

Salvation Sermon

O God, Mighty Recycler, we remember Zacchaeus.
He was a little man up a tree—way out on a limb.
He was about to fall and get trashed, thrown away,
wasted. But then you spoke to him through the mouth
of Jesus: "Make haste, come down, I must stay at your
house!" And so he was saved, and refurbished, for
a new life of service to his fellow human beings.

O God, who is in the reclamation business and yet
who is always about to get wasted, save us from the
dump, we pray. Polish us up and use us as shining
evidence of your deep desire that no one or no thing
should be lost. AMEN.

Vocation

Thank you, O God, for putting us in this garden of opportunity. We want to help you. Honestly, we do. Some of us hear you calling us to vocation of parent and homemaker. Some of us feel drawn to the life of the mind, to scholarship and teaching. Some groove on law, some on music or medicine. Some of us are still listening and waiting, muddling along, open to new adventures as you lead us.

Whatever we do with our lives, O God, may they be a blessing to others. Help us to help people find meaning and purpose, love and life.

God, if it be your will, gift us to be part of such miracles of the spirit wherever we can. Thus, we will have lived out our vocations and found in your garden the fullness of our own lives.

In Jesus' name, we pray. AMEN.

Peace is Possible

Thanks to God that peace is possible.

You waste nothing, O God. You use it all in the
cause of peace. You can even use our shadow sides,
our feelings of violence, our dislike of ourselves, by
helping us know that, precisely in our imperfection
and our limitedness, we can carry on our ministries
of reconciliation.

Fill all our nooks and crannies with new energies
for your cause of peace, O Lord. AMEN.

Students

O God, whose faithful disciples have searched your
word for millennia now—sometimes wearing ragged
clothes and milling in desert places, sometimes sitting
muffled up in cold libraries of stone where the books
were chained to the desks, sometimes in front of ghetto
shops peering through thick lenses, sometimes in
furtive glimpses in the upper bunks at Auschwitz—it is
our turn now, sitting in comfort at tables.

We praise you for so rich a heritage. We ask you to
empower us to give to this task no less zeal than theirs,
and we cry with them. O send out your light and truth!
Through He whose light guided us here. AMEN.

Yale Divinity School Prayer

O God—who has always lifted women and men
out of the mire of the mundane, out of the hell of
hopelessness, by visions of what we might become
in your kingdom through our study of the promises
of scripture and the preaching of the church about
ultimate things—help us to experience more fully the
brightness of that destiny toward which you are pulling
us. Even your city—even Jerusalem, O God.

O God, you have entrusted to us great adult
responsibilities: the safety of the other creatures,
the condition of the topsoil and the purity of the water,
the integrity of human relationships, the formation of
the outlooks of children, the honor and care of the
aged. And God, you have given us rules, too—truth
and fair play, reason and honor, trust in your power
and in our own powers, and love.

There is no turning back. The way leads only ahead.
We can go that way, O God, with your help and
presence in our midst.

Help us, O God, we pray, to attain the fullness of the
human stature that you gave us. Help us, we pray, to
go on to the perfection in giving which our natures
long to achieve. Help us, O God, to be like you in our
providential outpouring of love toward the other people
and the other creatures with whom we share this world.

Then, if our nose is crooked or our hair is stringy or we sustained neurological damage at birth or we are poor or we sometimes think nasty, violent thoughts, it won't matter very much. We will be fulfilling the destiny which you gave us—to love just like you do.

Maybe Jesus wanted to put the finishing touches on our happiness, O God, when he said, *"makarioi hoi katharoi te kardia"*—"Happy are the pure in heart, for they shall see God."

But purity of heart is to will one thing—utter loyalty to your sovereign lordship, O God, and toward all who are your people. Strengthen our hearts, we pray, to love you and yours with a fierce totality, and so complete our happiness and fill this place with joy. AMEN.

The Last Day

Almighty God, give us the grace to avoid the darkness
and to participate in those radiant enterprises of
rescuing and rejoicing done in this world in the name
of Jesus Christ. And on the last day, when the son
of man shall come in glorious majesty to banish all
darkness, evil, and death forever, may we and all
humankind stand before him in gratitude and peace.

In Christ's name, we pray. AMEN.

Why We Love Jesus

Let us remember why we love Jesus above all others:

because he loved the sick and the disordered, using
for other people the power that he would not invoke
for himself;

because he refused to force anyone's allegiance
with threats or bribes;

because he prayed for forgiveness for those
who rejected him, and for the perfecting of those
who received him;

because he honored tradition, yet set aside
conventions that did not serve God's purpose.

O Christ, our Savior, dwell within us in your Spirit, so
that we may go forth with the light of hope in our eyes,
and with the very passion of your love in our hearts.
AMEN.

64576985R10066

Made in the USA
Middletown, DE
15 February 2018